MW00483190

Carole Addlestone

Many Paths ONE Truth

The Common Thread

Carole Addlestone

Many
Paths
ONE
Truth

The Common Thread

Humanics Ltd.
Atlanta

Humanics Trade
PO Box 7400
Atlanta, GA 30357
USA

Humanics Trade is an imprint of Humanics Ltd.

Copyright © 1997 by Humanics Ltd.
All rights reserved. No part of this book may be reproduced by any means, nor transmitted, nor translated into a machine language, without written permission from Humanics Trade. Humanics Trade specifically reserves Moral Rights to this book.

First Edition

PRINTED IN THE UNITED STATES OF AMERICA

Library of Congress Cataloging-in-Publication Data

Many paths, one truth: the common thread/ [compiled by] Carole
    Addlestone. - 1st ed.
        p.   cm.
    Includes bibliographical references.
    ISBN 0-89334-248-3 (pbk.)
    1. Religions - Quotations, maxims, etc. I. Addlestone, Carole,
    1945-
    BL80.2.M2866   1996
    291.8 - dc20   96-33087

CIP

To my parents
and
ultimate Parent

There is no truth superior to Me. Everything rests upon Me, as pearls are strung on a thread.

— *Bhagavad-Gita*

CONTENTS

Preface viii

Acknowledgments x

Introduction 1

1. Faith 10

2. Trust 14

3. Courage 18

4. Giving 22

5. Golden Rule 26

6. Brotherhood 30

7. Conflict 34

8. Friends 38

9. Family 42

10. Love 46

11. Happiness 50

12. Contemplation 54

13. Gratitude 58

14. Truthfulness 62

15. Humbleness 66

16. Obedience 70

17. Duty 74

18. Work 78

19. Deeds 82

20. Justice 86

21. Forgiveness 90

22. Prosperity 94

23. Human and Divine 98

24. Immortality 102

Afterword 106

Bibliography 107

PREFACE

In the world of God there are no religions. "People partition off their lands by means of boundaries, but no one can partition off the all-embracing sky overhead. The indivisible sky surrounds all and includes all." [1] In the Divine world there are only God — the Creator of the universe, heaven, and earth — and the eternal principles and laws set in motion by His Love, Will, and Wisdom. God, our Parent, has granted life to all existence, breathing His energy, the Light, into each living thing and into every human soul. We are truly children of God. He is the origin of all, the center, the core, the Truth that we each seek to make sense of our lives and destinies.

Religions, however, are vital manifestations of humankind's diverse paths to strive for the Divine and for the divinity in each of us. The Hindu master Shri Ramakrishna put it this way: "To get a crop one needs to sow the grain with the husk on. But if one wants to get at the kernel itself, he must remove the husk of the grain. So rites and ceremonies are necessary for the growth and the perpetuation of a religion. They are the receptacles that contain the kernel of truth, and consequently every man must perform them before he reaches the central truth..." [2] It is with this in mind that I highlight eight great living religions, which have evolved over many centuries of human civilization and culture and whose rich contributions are deeply interwoven in the fabric of our existence. They originated in different ages and different lands, yet there is a common thread, as shown through the excerpts presented here. In a small volume such as this, the ethical and spiritual profundity of the teachings of each of these religions cannot be approached or, perhaps, even imagined. It is my hope, however, that the reader can at least taste the wonderful diversity of traditions and yet savor their dynamic core — the essential oneness that bonds all humanity.

In these chaotic times when religious intolerance and fanaticism are creating conflicts around the globe and our materialistically oriented society and culture have not provided adequate nourishment for the soul, humankind has not been able to perceive its center. This is because it has pushed it far away and instead summoned a condition of division and disharmony. Humankind has divorced itself from God's Will and the laws of the universe. When one forgets the center, things break down. From the center of the universe comes order and thus the foundation of civilization and culture upon which religions can flourish.

Do we not long to return to our origin, the center? How can we eliminate the gap between God and humankind? How can we tune in, or harmonize, with the Will of God? Should we not live life in a righteous way, with gratitude for all our blessings and apology for all our shortcomings? These sacred writings were selected to address these significant questions. It is my earnest prayer that this book be an instrument to foster respect for the role of religion in our society and, even more, that the Truth underlying all religions be recognized so that humankind can unite in love and harmony and make effort to create a God-centered civilization in the twenty-first century, a flourishing civilization where material resources are governed by spiritual wisdom and one religion — the Divine Truth — sustains all.

Through these pages may we be permitted to deeply discern that the origin of the world is one, the origin of humankind is one, all religions have the same origin. I hope you enjoy this exploration as much as I have.

[1] (sayings of Ramakrishna) Brian Brown, *The Wisdom of the Hindus* (Albuquerque, NM: Sun Books, 1981), 265.
[2] (sayings of Ramakrishna) Editorial staff of *Life* magazine. *The World's Great Religions: Vol 1: Religions of the East* (New York: Time, Inc., 1963), 46-47.

ACKNOWLEDGMENTS

With heartfelt gratitude I thank the following:

The authors, translators, and editors whose writings comprise this book. (Please note that for the convenience of the reader wording has been slightly changed, in some cases, for accuracy and clarity and/or anglicized; and spelling and punctuation have been standardized for consistency and for conformity with common Western usage.)

Tameko Roberts and Yoshimi Ueda for their translations.

Gerald Ardis for his invaluable research assistance.

Donna Gates and Heather Grant for their special friendship, spiritual encouragement, and suggestions.

Barbara Norgren and Loraine Fick, who so generously and cheerfully handled my regular work assignments in order to give me extra time to concentrate on this project.

Dean and Jean Logan for their computer assistance in the organization of the manuscript.

Adrian Fillion, Edward Fierman, Heather Spahr, and Susan Addlestone Berlijn for their editorial input.

My family and friends for their kind encouragement all along the way.

INTRODUCTION

EIGHT RELIGIONS OF THE WORLD

The eight religions — Hinduism, Buddhism, Taoism, Confucianism, Zoroastrianism, Judaism, Christianity, and Islam — are very briefly presented here simply to give a point of reference for the excerpts of their writings that follow.

For the most part, these excerpts were selected from what is considered sacred literature to each of these religions. I have used "primary" sources, such as the *Koran*, whenever possible, but also some "secondary" sources, such as paraphrased teachings — for example, in Buddhism and Judaism — that shed light on "original" teachings inasmuch as we can know them.

There are, of course, many difficulties inherent in this process of selection. For one, which teachings and rituals within a religion best represent it? In Buddhism, Hinayana or Mahayana? In Islam, Sunnah or Shiah? What about Roman Catholicism, Anglican and Eastern Orthodox churches, and the many sects of Protestantism — all under the banner of Christianity?

Related to this concern is the question of what are the actual original teachings of the founder or early exponents of each of these religions. Most of their words come filtered down to us through their disciples and followers and, in some cases, reformers. And these come to us through translators and with varying interpretations. And in the particular case of Shinto (meaning "Way of the Gods"), a major religion native to Japan that dates back to prehistoric times, it was impossible to present meaningfully here the teachings (although the rites and ceremonies of current Shinto are widely observed) of the ancient pure form of this faith, because extremely few writings are known to exist and, of those that do, very little has been translated into the English language.

And what is perhaps most interesting to contemplate, some of the founders of these religions never considered starting a religion and did not expect or even imagine that they would be idolized and worshipped in a formal way by adherents through the ages.

1

Hinduism

Hinduism dates from a period between 2000 and 1500 B.C. and is regarded as the world's oldest organized religion. The words "Hinduism" and "Hindu" come from the Sanskrit word "sindhu," which means "river."

A religion and social system native to India, Hinduism began as mostly polytheistic worship but gradually developed into monism, a concept in which all reality and existences are regarded as one. Hindus believe that everything, including humankind, is Brahman, the Absolute, the eternal spirit; to unite with Brahman through their ritual and ethics is their goal. There have been several reform movements within the religion, and many of the modern faithful do not adhere to Hindu doctrines in their earliest form.

The most important writings, the hymns of the *Rig Veda* — dating from about 1500 -1000 B.C., derived from a long oral tradition. Nature worship is chiefly reflected in these hymns. Later, possibly from the second century B.C. to the second century A.D., the renowned *Bhagavad-Gita* was composed.

Today there are about 751,360,000 Hindus.

Buddhism

Buddhism originated in India and is considered as a reform within Hinduism, or response to Hindu asceticism extremes. Buddhism's worldwide membership is 334,002,000, but only about one-half million now live in India.

Gautama, the founder of Buddhism, lived in the sixth and early fifth centuries B.C. (his year of birth commonly given as 567 B.C. and year of death as 483 B.C.). He was from the Shakya clan and often called Shakyamuni. When he was twenty-nine, he rejected his life of wealth and worldly abundance, left his home and family, and set forth as a homeless wanderer to seek peace and truth.

Later on, he was called the Buddha, meaning the "Enlightened One." He taught that to detach from desire was the source of salvation, and he advocated a life of moderation that would follow the Noble Eightfold Path: right views, right aspirations, right speech, right conduct, right livelihood, right effort, right mindfulness, and right concentration. It is believed that the practice of this path can lead to total enlightenment.

In its early phases, Buddhism could not be called a religion but a philosophy and moral system. As time progressed, many miracle stories were told about Buddha's life, he became deified, and Buddhism was classified as a religion.

There are many sects of Buddhism and two major divisions: Mahayana and Hinayana. Mahayana, "the Greater Vehicle," is the Buddhism of Northeast Asia (China, Japan, Korea, Tibet, Mongolia); it "stands for salvation by faith and good works." [1] Here, monastic life is the way to spread Buddhism to laymen. With Mahayana, many myths were added and the supernatural elements of Buddhism heightened. Hinayana, "the Lesser Vehicle," is the Buddhism of Southeast Asia (Cambodia, Laos, Ceylon, Burma, Thailand); it glorifies personal asceticism, the monastic life as the best way of life, and "salvation by personal example." [2]

The *Tripitaka* are the earliest sacred writings, set down by the first century B.C. and possibly even in the third century B.C. One section of this work is the *Sattapitaka*, which expounds Buddha's teachings.

Taoism

Taoism is one of the three major religions of China (the other two being Confucianism and Buddhism). Its chief literature is the *Tao Te Ching*, traditionally attributed to the philosopher Lao Tzu, an older contemporary of Confucius. Lao Tzu is generally believed to have lived in the sixth century B.C.; however, the style of the *Tao Te Ching* indicates he may have lived during the third century, even though it is not known if he or a later writer/writers actually authored it.

"Tao Te Ching" means the "Classic of the Way (Tao) and Power/Virtue (Te)" — the ethical way of humankind and the way of the universe and principles of nature. Originally a philosophy, Taoism later developed in the direction of magic (the practice of Feng Shui for gravesites was related to this), a hierarchy of deities was set forth, and a religion organized near the time of the start of the Christian era.

Taoism as an organized religion no longer exists in mainland China as it does in Taiwan, because its priests were coerced to return to the lay life. No figures are currently available as to the number of modern adherents.

Confucianism

The official religion of China is Confucianism, even though it is regarded more as a system of ethics or philosophy than as a religion. Its founder, Confucius (551-479 B.C.), did not consider his *Analects* (sayings attributed to him but not actually written down by him) a religious work but a social and political commentary. During his career as a government administrator, he became renowned for rules of courtesy and humane behavior. Later, he dedicated himself to teaching and writing. Although he had belief in spiritual matters, Confucius was not principally a religious leader. His chief concern was how to organize and reform society in harmony with ethical principles.

In time he was venerated as a god due to his life and works, and the religion called Confucianism developed.

The number of followers of modern Confucianism is estimated at 250,000,000.

Zoroastrianism

Zoroastrianism evolved on the Iranian plateau and was founded by Zoroaster (the Greek form of his name), or Zarathustra (as his name appears in ancient Avestan). There is controversy still as to the dates of his life, although the most likely ones are 570 - 493 B.C.

Zoroaster had his first visions at the age of thirty. Then, he strove to reform the ancient Persian religion of his time. In his middle years he founded temples across the land.

Characterized by a substantial tendency toward monotheism and by a cosmic and moral dualism of good and evil and human accountability and also by the concept of a Last Judgment, Zoroastrianism has profoundly influenced Judaism, Christianity, and Islam.

The original writings of the religion are contained in the *Avesta*. It is a possibility that Zoroaster himself composed the *Gathas*, which comprise the central part of the *Yasna* (one of the five primary sections of the *Avesta*), due to the fact they are written in archaic Avestan.

Ironically (in view of his monotheistic perspective), Zoroaster came to be considered a god and was worshipped as Zoroastrianism evolved, and many myths and miracle stories relating to his birth and life were created. The religion also was transformed by polytheistic and magic influences.

There is a remnant of about 20,000 Zoroastrians in Iran; others, called Parsis, left in the seventh and eighth centuries for India, where there are still about 120,000 adherents, mostly in Bombay.

Judaism

Judaism is known as the religion of the Hebrews. From its beginnings with a Sumero-Babylonian influence and a Semitic heritage of animism and polytheistic beliefs, monotheism evolved slowly. In its long history of development from prior to 1200 B.C., Judaism has adapted much from, as well as greatly influenced, many other faiths.

Judaism emphasizes the need to keep the law, justice, God's mercy, and the prime importance of love toward God and humankind. Among its sacred literature, it has given to the world the Old Testament, which includes the *Torah* (regarded as the five books of Moses), the great legacy of the ethical tradition from the prophets, and the *Talmud* (completed by the end of the fifth century B.C.), a collection of ancient rabbinic writings.

Modern Judaism includes the Orthodox, Conservative, Reform, and Reconstructionist movements, and together their worldwide membership is about 12,850,000.

Christianity

As the Dead Sea Scrolls reveal, the origin of Christian concepts was associated with the Jewish Essene tradition. The Essenes practiced baptism and asceticism, and believed in the immortality of the soul and in the universe as the scene of a duel between the forces of light and darkness. John the Baptist; Mary, mother of Jesus; as well as Jesus, were all related to the Essene sect.

Jesus was a Jew and imbued with Jewish law, culture, and tradition. In his ministry, Jesus stressed the importance of an ethical way of life based on love as fulfillment of the law, service to others, and forgiveness. Jesus and his disciples diverged from a narrow interpretation of Jewish law and preached the moral idealism of the great prophets to all, Jew and non-Jew alike.

Paul's letter to the Galatians is regarded by scholars as the first book of the New Testament to be written (probably in A.D. 49). By A.D. 400, the New Testament scriptures were authorized as canon.

During the time of the Roman Empire, Christianity grew into a religious movement. Throughout the history of the Christian church, there have been schisms, and many sects and denominations have been established. Missionaries have traveled to the far corners of the earth to relay Christianity's message, and today there are about 1,869,751,000 adherents worldwide.

Islam

Islam, which means "submission" (to the Will of God), originated in Arabia from the time of its founder Mohammed's migration from Mecca to Medina in A.D. 622. Mohammed was born around A.D. 570 and received his first revelation about A.D. 609. He gave the world the *Koran* (*Qur'an*, a noun from the verb *qaru'a*, "to read," "to discourse," or "to rewrite"), although it is generally established that he did not write it down himself.

A monotheistic faith, Islam proclaims it is based upon the original religion of Abraham. Its five pillars are: reciting the creed, praying five times a day, giving alms, fasting during the month of Ramadan, and making pilgrimage to Mecca.

There are two major sects of Islam, the Sunnites and the Shi'ites; the Sufis are the mystic sect. The Sunnites are the traditionalist, or orthodox, sect, which accepts the first four caliphs as legitimate successors of Mohammed. The Shi'ites comprise the sect that follows Ali, the cousin and son-in-law of Mohammed. They consider Ali's heirs rightful successors to Mohammed and do not accept other caliphs and the legal and political institutions of the Sunnites. Originally an ascetic order, the Sufi sect dates from the eighth century. Its major interest was union with God in the present life instead of after death. Its members practice prescribed periods of meditation.

In Islam today, there are approximately 1,014,375,000 believers throughout the world.

* * *

With the diverse backgrounds of these religions in mind, let us turn to the specific topics in the following chapters to experience not only the colorful differences of these sacred writings but also, and especially, the common thread --- the Divine Truth --- that binds them all, one to another.

[1,2] Editorial staff of *Life* magazine. *The World's Great Religions: Vol.1: Religions of the East* (New York: Time, Inc., 1963), 51.

Chapter One

FAITH

Hinduism

He who has faith has all, and he who lacks faith lacks all.
As a lamp does not burn without oil, so man cannot live without God.

Buddhism

Faith is the wealth here best for man; by faith the flood is crossed.

On the long journey of human life, faith is the best of companions, faith is the
best refreshment by the way and the greatest reward at the end...
faith brings one to enlightenment.

Taoism

When righteousness is lost, there are rites.
Rites are only the shell of faith and loyalty and the beginning of disorder.

Confucianism

Confucius said, "If people have no faith, I don't know what they are good for.
Can a vehicle travel without a link to a source of power?"

Zoroastrianism

But whoso...unites his conscience with the Good Mind [Providence],
O Wise One,
Whoso is, through Righteousness, a knight of Devotion,
For all those there shall be a place in Thy Dominion, O Lord!

Judaism

Behold, he whose soul is not upright in him shall fail, but the righteous shall
live by his faith.

Christianity

For in it [the gospel] the righteousness of God is revealed through faith for faith;
as it is written, "He who through faith is righteous shall live."

"For truly, I say to you, if you have faith as a grain of mustard seed, you will
say to this mountain, 'Move from here to there,' and it will move;
and nothing will be impossible to you."

Islam

Surely they that believe...whoso believes in God and the Last Day, and works in
righteousness — their wage awaits them with their Lord, and
no fear shall be on them; neither shall they sorrow.

PERSONAL NOTES

Chapter Two

TRUST

Hinduism

No enemies can overcome the believer. He trusts in God,
knowing that God will guide him through all troubles.

Buddhism

The mind of faith...is a deep mind, an unquestioning mind.

Taoism

One who loves himself as much as the world
can be trusted with the world.

Confucianism

Confucius said, "If you are truthful, you will be trusted."

Zoroastrianism

What help shall my soul expect from anyone,
In whom am I to put my trust...
But in the Right, in Thee, Wise Lord, and the Best Mind [Providence]?

Judaism

The Lord is a stronghold for the oppressed, a stronghold in times of trouble; and
those who know Thy name put their trust in Thee,
for Thou, O Lord, hast not forsaken those who seek Thee.

Christianity

If one trusts in God, He will carry him through all hardship and troubles.
One should have complete confidence in God. Even in persecution
one should not falter, for God will guide him to his reward.

Islam

If God helps you, none can overcome you; but if He forsakes you, who then can
help you after Him? Therefore, in God let the believers put all their trust.

PERSONAL NOTES

Chapter Three

COURAGE

Hinduism

Virtue is the best of friends; vice is the worst of enemies; disappointment
is the cruelest of illnesses; courage is the support of all.

Buddhism

Faith gives one courage to meet hardship;
faith gives one power to overcome temptation.

Taoism

One with courage and daring will be killed.
One with courage and gentleness will survive.
One yields benefit; the other yields harm.

Confucianism

Confucius said, "Humanitarians are courageous,
but the courageous are not necessarily humane."

The Master said, "...To see what is right and not to do it is lack of courage."

Zoroastrianism

Courage begets strength by struggle with hardships. Courage grows from
fighting danger and overcoming obstacles. Develop the courage to act according
to your convictions, to speak what is true, and to do what is right.

Judaism

Have I not commanded you? Be strong and of good courage; be not frightened, neither be dismayed, for the Lord, your God, is with you wherever you go.

Christianity

So we are always of good courage; we know that while we are at home in the body we are away from the Lord, for we walk by faith, not by sight. We are of good courage, and we would rather be away from the body and at home with the Lord. So whether we are at home or away, we make it our aim to please Him.

Islam

God will guide the good; therefore, they shall have no fear. He will lead them through all the difficult times of life.

PERSONAL NOTES

Chapter Four

GIVING

Hinduism

The gift lovingly given — when one shall say, "Now must I gladly give!" when he who takes can render nothing back — made in due place, in due time, and to a meet recipient, is a gift...fair and profitable.

Buddhism

If one gives a gift only after he has been importuned or because it is easier to give than not to give, it is charity, of course, but it is not true Charity. True Charity is given freely from a sympathetic heart before any request has been made, and true Charity is not occasional but is constant. Neither is it true Charity if after the act there are feelings of regret or self-praise; true Charity is given with pleasure — one forgetting himself as the giver, forgetting the one who has received the gift and the gift itself. True Charity springs spontaneously from a merciful heart, with no thought of any return or of any inconvenience or even of life itself, desiring only that others may enter with the self into a life of Enlightenment.

Taoism

The sage does not accumulate things.
The more he does for others, the more he has.
The more he gives to others, the more he receives.

Confucianism

When Confucius was an official of Lu, one of his disciples served as his steward. Confucius gave him nine hundred measures of grain, but the disciple refused. Confucius said, "Don't refuse. Why not give it to your neighbors?"

Zoroastrianism

The Wise One was generous, so should all His followers be generous. To the
extent that one helps the poor, one helps to make the Lord King.

Judaism

One man gives freely, yet grows all the richer; another withholds what he
should give and only suffers want. A liberal man will be enriched,
and one who waters will himself be watered.

Christianity

Each one must do as he has made up his mind to do, not reluctantly or under
compulsion, for God loves a cheerful giver. And God is able to provide you
with every blessing in abundance, so that you may always have enough of
everything and may provide in abundance for every good work. As it is written,
"He scatters abroad, he gives to the poor; his righteousness endures forever."

Islam

True piety is this...to give of one's substance, however cherished, to kinsmen,
and orphans, the needy, the traveller, and beggars, and to ransom the slave, to
perform the prayer, to pay the alms.

PERSONAL NOTES

Chapter Five

GOLDEN RULE

Hinduism

Do not to others what would be disagreeable to yourself.

Buddhism

If one wishes to follow the Buddha's teaching, he must not be egoistic or self-willed, but should cherish feelings of good will toward all alike. He should respect those who are worthy of respect, serve those who are worthy of service, and treat all others with uniform kindness.

Taoism

He who will govern will respect the governed no more than he respects himself. If he loves his own person enough to let it rest in its original truth, he will govern others without hurting them.

Confucianism

Confucius said, "What you do not want done to yourself, do not do to others."

Zoroastrianism

That nature alone is good which shall not do unto another whatever is not good for its own self.

Judaism

You shall not take vengeance or bear any grudge against the sons of your own people, but you shall love your neighbor as yourself.

When a stranger sojourns with you in your land, you shall not do him wrong. The stranger who sojourns with you shall be to you as the native among you, and you shall love him as yourself.

Christianity

So whatever you wish that men would do to you, do so to them; for this is the law and the prophets.

Owe others nothing, except to love one another; for he who loves his neighbor has fulfilled the law..."You shall love your neighbor as yourself." Love does no wrong to a neighbor; therefore, love is the fulfilling of the law.

Islam

Wrong not, and ye shall not be wronged.

PERSONAL NOTES

Chapter Six

BROTHERHOOD

Hinduism

The good man makes no distinction between friend and foe, brother and stranger, but regards them all with impartiality.

Buddhism

The rain of the sacred teaching falls on all people alike without regard to their conditions and circumstances...Enlightened minds mix like milk and water and quickly organize into a harmonious Brotherhood.

Taoism

The spirit of brotherhood, kindness, is necessary for one to win friends.

Confucianism

"Let the superior man never fail reverentially to order his own conduct, and let him be respectful to others and observant of propriety; then all within the four seas will be his brothers..."

The Master said, "It [Benevolence] is to love all men."

Zoroastrianism

A holy man will radiate holiness to all his brethren.

Judaism

If there is among you a poor man, one of your brethren, in any of your towns within your land which the Lord, your God, gives you, you shall not harden your heart or shut your hand against your poor brother, but you shall open your hand to him and lend him that which is sufficient for his need, whatever it may be.

May we learn to know that in loving and serving our fellowmen, we are loving and serving Thee.

O may all created in Thine image recognize that they are brethren, so that, one in spirit and one in fellowship, they may be forever united before Thee.

Christianity

If anyone says, "I love God," and hates his brother, he is a liar; for he who does not love his brother, whom he has seen, cannot love God, whom he has not seen. And this commandment we have from Him, that he who loves God should love his brother, also.

Let brotherly love continue. Do not neglect to show hospitality to strangers, for thereby some have entertained angels unawares.

Islam

No one of you is a believer until he loves for his brother what he loves for himself.

PERSONAL NOTES

Chapter Seven

CONFLICT

Hinduism

Dispute not. As you rest firmly on your own faith and opinion, allow others...to stand by their own faiths and opinions. By mere disputation you will never succeed in convincing another of his error. When the grace of God descends upon him, he will understand his own mistakes. As long as the bee is outside the petals of the lily and has not tasted the sweetness of its honey, it hovers around the flower, emitting its buzzing sound; but when it is inside the flower, it noiselessly drinks its nectar. As long as a man quarrels and disputes about doctrines and dogmas, he has not tasted the nectar of true faith.
When he has tasted it, he becomes quiet and full of peace.

Buddhism

Under my teachings, brothers should respect each other and refrain from disputes; they should not repel each other like water and oil, but should mingle together like milk and water, study together, learn together, and practice the teachings together. Do not waste your mind and time in idleness and bickering.
Enjoy the blossoms of enlightenment in their season,
and harvest the fruit of benevolence.

He, truly, is supreme in battle,
Who would conquer himself alone,
Rather than he who would conquer in battle
A thousand, thousand men.

Taoism

A good captain does not exhibit his martial prowess.
A good warrior does not get himself angry.
A good conqueror of enemies does not instigate a combat.
A good employer of people puts himself below them.
This is called the power of non-contention.

Because he does not contend with anyone,
Therefore no one under heaven can contend with him.

Confucianism

Confucius said, "Cultivated people do not contend over anything."

Zoroastrianism

Let fury be suppressed! Put down violence,
You who would ensure yourselves, through Righteousness,
The reward of the Good Mind [Providence], whose companion is the holy man.
He shall have his abode in Thy house, O Lord!

Judaism

A soft answer turns away wrath, but a harsh word stirs up anger.

A hot-tempered man stirs up strife, but he who is slow to anger
quiets contention.

He who is slow to anger is better than the mighty, and he who rules his spirit
than he who takes a city.

Christianity

Let all bitterness and wrath and anger and clamor and slander be put away
from you, with all malice, and be kind to one another, tenderhearted,
forgiving one another.

Islam

Aggress not; God loves not the aggressors.

Chapter Eight

FRIENDS

Hinduism

There is naught better than to be
With noble souls in company;
There is naught better than to wend
With good friends faithful to the end.

That friend only is the true friend who abides when trouble comes.

Buddhism

Let one not associate
With low persons, bad friends.
...But let one associate
With noble persons, worthy friends.

A true friend, the one with whom a man may safely associate, will always advise sticking closely to the right way, will worry secretly about his friend's welfare, will console him in misfortune, will offer him a helping hand when he needs it, and will always give him good advice. It is very hard to find a friend like this. As the sun warms the fruitful earth, so a good friend stimulates a man.

Taoism

Good words shall gain you honor in the marketplace, but good deeds shall gain you friends among men.

Confucianism

Confucius said, "Three kinds of friends are beneficial, and three are harmful. When friends are honest, sincere, or knowledgeable, they are beneficial. When friends are pretentious, fawning, or opportunistic, they are harmful."

Zoroastrianism

The good should associate with those whom they can help. A virtuous man will radiate his virtue far and wide. One is fortunate to be the associate of such a good man.

Judaism

There are friends who pretend to be friends, but there is a friend who sticks closer than a brother.

Christianity

"This is my commandment, that you love one another as I have loved you. Greater love has no man than this, that a man lay down his life for his friends."

Islam

You should act toward your friends honorably; that stands inscribed in the Book.

PERSONAL NOTES

Chapter Nine

FAMILY

Hinduism

He who feeds us is our father; he who helps us is our brother; he who places his confidence in us is our friend; those whose sentiments accord with ours are our kinsmen.

Buddhism

A family is a place where a mind lives with other minds. If these minds love each other, the home will be as beautiful as a flower garden. But if these minds get out of harmony with each other, it is like a storm that plays havoc with a garden. If discord arises within one's family, one should not blame others but should examine his own mind and follow a right path.

Taoism

Discard [artificial] morality and its righteousness, and
People will return to family duty and love.

One who is well established is not uprooted,
One who embraces firmly cannot be separated from...

In cultivating this in one's person,
The person's *te* [virtue] becomes genuine;
In cultivating this in the family,
The family's *te* has more to spare;
In cultivating this in the village,
The village's *te* grows strong;
In cultivating this in the state,
The state's *te* becomes abundant;
In cultivating this in the world,
The world's *te* becomes universal.

Confucianism

By acquiring the right attitude, they [the ancients who desired to set an example of good character] developed themselves.
By developing themselves, they guided their families.
By guiding their families, they established moral order in their states.
By establishing moral order in their states, they brought peace and prosperity to the whole country.

Confucius said, "...That a son should love his parents is fate — you cannot erase this from his heart...Therefore, to serve your parents and be content to follow them anywhere — this is the perfection of filial piety."

Zoroastrianism

Those who act in accordance with the wishes of their parents and respect them do the equivalent of prayer to God.

Judaism

Honor your father and your mother, that your days may be long in the land which the Lord, your God, gives you.

A righteous man who walks in his integrity — blessed are his sons after him!

Christianity

While he was still speaking to the people, behold, his mother and his brothers stood outside, asking to speak to him. But he replied to the man who told him, "Who is my mother, and who are my brothers?" And stretching out his hand toward his disciples, he said, "Here are my mother and my brothers! For whoever does the will of my Father in heaven is my brother, and sister, and mother."

Islam

Be good to parents, whether one or both of them attain old age with thee; say not "Fie" nor chide them, but speak unto them words respectful, and lower to them the wing of humbleness out of mercy and say, "My Lord, have mercy upon them, as they raised me up when I was little."

Chapter Ten

LOVE

Hinduism

In each individual heart a stream of love is flowing, which like a confined river constantly seeks an outlet through which it can run into that ocean of Divine Love, which is called God.

Father's love should recognize that Ideal as his child. Mother's love should see It in her newborn babe. The love of a brother or of a sister should establish a fraternal relationship with It. A husband who is devoted to his wife should think of his Eternal Ideal in the soul of his wife, and a wife should put her highest spiritual Ideal in the soul of her beloved husband and love him with her whole heart and soul. The love of a friend should look upon It as his dearest friend and the Divine Companion. In this way all earthly relationships could be spiritualized and all human affection could in the course of time be transformed into expressions of Divine Love in daily life. There would be no more cause of dissatisfaction in a household, no more fighting between brothers and sisters, no more divorce on account of incompatibility of temper. Then each of these human affections would be like a path that leads to Divine Reality and eternal happiness.

Buddhism

One act of pure love in saving life is greater than spending the whole of one's time in religious offerings to the gods.

Taoism

Love finds what sages seek. Body and mind disappear. Division and separation end. The Being that is all overcomes the thinking that is some.

Confucianism

Love makes a spot beautiful — who chooses not to dwell in love, has he got wisdom? Love is the high nobility of Heaven, the peaceful home of man. To lack love, when nothing hinders us, is to lack wisdom. Lack of love and wisdom leads to lack of courtesy and right, and without these man is a slave.

Zoroastrianism

There is one thing that every man in this world below may love...
he may love Virtue.

Man is the beloved of the Lord and should love Him in return.

Judaism

Thou shalt love the Lord, thy God, with all thy heart, with all thy soul, and with all thy might. And these words, which I command thee this day, shall be upon thy heart. Thou shalt teach them diligently unto thy children, and shalt speak of them when thou sittest in thy house, when thou walkest by the way, when thou liest down, and thou risest up. Thou shalt bind them for a sign upon thy hand, and they shall be for frontlets between thine eyes. Thou shalt write them upon the doorposts of thy house and upon thy gates: That ye may remember and do all My commandments and be holy unto your God.

Infinite as is Thy power, even so is Thy love.

Christianity

"You shall love the Lord, your God, with all your heart, and with all your soul, and with all your mind. This is the great and first commandment. And a second is like it: You shall love your neighbor as yourself. On these two commandments depend all the law and the prophets."

Let us love one another; for love is of God, and he who loves is born of God and knows God. He who does not love does not know God; for God is love...No man has ever seen God; if we love one another, God abides in us and His love is perfected in us. By this we know that we abide in Him and He in us, because He has given us of His own Spirit...We love, because He first loved us.

Islam

Surely unto those who believe and do deeds of righteousness
the All-merciful shall assign love.

Chapter Eleven

HAPPINESS

Hinduism

"Which is the way to be happy?"
"To say the truth and be kind."

One whose self is not attached to external objects obtains the happiness that is in one's self; and by concentration of mind, joining one's self with the Brahman [the Absolute], one obtains indestructible happiness.

Buddhism

If a man speaks and acts from a good mind, happiness follows him as a man's shadow...those who act from good motives are made happy by the thought, "I have done a good act," and are made happier by the thought that the good act will bring continuing happiness in endless lives to follow.

Taoism

Human happiness comes from perfect harmony with one's fellow beings.
The source of divine happiness is complete accord with God.
The good shall be truly happy.

Confucianism

Confucius said, "The knowing enjoy water; the humane enjoy mountains. The knowing are diligent; the humane are quiet. The knowing are happy, the humane are long-lived."

Zoroastrianism

Holiness is the source of the truest happiness. Only those who live justly shall know happiness. The unrighteousness of man shall bring misery.

Judaism

Happy is the man who finds wisdom and the man who gets understanding... Her [Wisdom's] ways are ways of pleasantness, and all her paths are peace. She is a tree of life to those who lay hold of her; those who hold her fast are called happy.

Happy is he whose help is the God of Jacob, whose hope is in the Lord, his God, Who made heaven and earth, the sea, and all that is in them; who keeps faith forever; who executes justice for the oppressed; who gives food to the hungry.

Christianity

Behold, we call those happy who were steadfast. You have heard of the steadfastness of Job, and you have seen the purpose of the Lord, how the Lord is compassionate and merciful.

Islam

As for the happy, they shall be in Paradise, therein dwelling forever, as long as the heavens and earth abide...

PERSONAL NOTES

Chapter Twelve

CONTEMPLATION

Hinduism

When one reflects, only then does one understand. One who does not reflect does not understand. Only one who reflects understands. One must desire to understand this reflection.

Make a habit of practicing meditation, and do not let your mind be distracted. In this way you will come finally to the Lord, who is the light-giver, the highest of the high.

Buddhism

Reflection is the path of immortality, a lack of reflection the path of death. Those who reflect do not die; those who do not reflect are as if dead already.

Through stillness joined to insight true,
...passions are annihilated.
Stillness must first of all be found.

Taoism

To a mind that is "still" the whole universe surrenders.

Confucianism

Man has three ways of acting wisely:
Firstly, on meditation --- this is the noblest;
Secondly, on imitation --- this is the costliest; and
Thirdly, on experience --- this is the bitterest.

Zoroastrianism

Keep the plan and purposes of the Lord always in mind. Meditate upon them day and night. Then you will come to clear understanding.

Judaism

At our lying down and our rising up, we will meditate on Thy teachings and find in Thy laws true life and length of days.

Christianity

Whatever is true, whatever is honorable, whatever is just, whatever is pure, whatever is lovely, whatever is gracious, if there is any excellence, if there is anything worthy of praise, think about these things.

Islam

It is He who sends down to you out of heaven water that you drink...thereby He brings forth for you crops, olives, palms, vines, and all manner of fruit. Surely in that is a sign for a people who reflect.

PERSONAL NOTES

Chapter Thirteen

GRATITUDE

Hinduism

The wise will remember throughout their sevenfold births the love of those who have wiped away the falling tear from their eyes. It is not good to forget a benefit; it is good to forget an injury even in the moment in which it is inflicted.

Buddhism

A person will add to his happiness by habits of recollection and reflection and thanksgiving.

Contentment is the highest wealth...

Taoism

There is...no calamity greater than to be discontented with one's lot, no fault greater than the wish to be getting. Therefore, the sufficiency of contentment is an enduring and unchanging sufficiency.

Confucianism

The Master said, "Admirable indeed was the virtue of Hui! With a single bamboo dish of rice, a single gourd dish of drink, and living in his mean narrow lane, while others could not have endured the distress, he did not allow his joy to be affected by it..."

Zoroastrianism

To be pleased over whatever God gives us, no matter how little or how much,
being happy over it, and showing gratitude to God for it —
this is the best meritorious deed.

Judaism

We gratefully acknowledge, O Lord, our God, that Thou art our Creator and
Preserver, the Rock of our life, and the Shield of our help. We render thanks
unto Thee for our lives which are in Thy hand, for our souls which are ever in
Thy keeping, for Thy wondrous providence and for Thy continuous goodness,
which Thou bestowest upon us day by day. Truly, Thy mercies never fail, and
Thy lovingkindness never ceases.

Teach us to be satisfied with the gifts of Thy goodness and gratefully to rejoice
in all Thy mercies.

Christianity

Be content with what you have, for He has said, "I will never fail you
nor forsake you."

Islam

It is He who made the sea your subject, that you may eat from it fresh flesh and
bring forth from it ornaments to wear; and thou mayest see the ships cleaving
through it; and that you may seek of His bounty,
and so haply you will be thankful.

PERSONAL NOTES

Chapter Fourteen

TRUTHFULNESS

Hinduism

Truth alone triumphs, not falsehood. By truth the path is laid out, the Way of the Gods.

In truth is the seat of immortality. Therefore, he who walks under the vows of truth and devotes himself to union with truth, and has a true scripture and is constantly self-controlled, overcomes death by the truth.

Buddhism

If you are consistent in speech and action, if you are guided by wisdom, if your mind is as resistant as a mountain, then you will make steady progress on the path to enlightenment.

Taoism

The manner of heaven is earnestness. If one is truthful and earnest in one's acts, one will attain genuine sainthood.

Confucianism

"Sincerity is the way of heaven. The attainment of sincerity is the way of men. He who possesses sincerity is he who, without an effort, hits what is right and apprehends without the exercise of thought; he is the sage who naturally and easily embodies the right way. He who attains to sincerity is he who chooses what is good and firmly holds it fast."

Zoroastrianism

A truth-speaker receives honor and is a master without fear.

By speaking true words we receive many rewards.

He who upholds Truth with all the might of his power,
He who upholds Truth to the utmost in his word and deed,
He, indeed, is the most valued helper, O Mazda Ahura [the Creator]!

Judaism

Blessed is the man to whom the Lord imputes no iniquity and in whose spirit there is no deceit.

Truthful lips endure forever, but a lying tongue is but for a moment.

Christianity

Let us not love in word or speech but in deed and in truth. By this we shall know that we are of the truth...

Islam

And they who fulfil their covenant when they have engaged in a covenant and who endure with fortitude misfortune, hardship, and peril are they who are true in their faith; they are the truly god-fearing.

PERSONAL NOTES

Chapter Fifteen

HUMBLENESS

Hinduism

Worship with a clean and lowly heart, keep a charitable spirit, do kindness according to your powers — this is the easy way to heaven.

Buddhism

The pure mind must at the same time be a deep mind, if it is to follow successfully the path to enlightenment. It must be the soul of compassion and charity, it must observe the precepts, it must be patient and humble,...it must be the soul of wisdom, as well as the soul of compassion, the soul that is earnest to use wise and kindly means and methods to bring all people to enlightenment.

Taoism

The exalted is rooted in the humble,
The high has the low for foundation.

Confucianism

The Master said, "The superior man in everything considers righteousness to be essential. He performs it according to the rules of propriety. He brings it forth in humility. He completes it with sincerity. This is indeed a superior man."

Zoroastrianism

He that in this world of the flesh...deemeth himself excessively proud of his own merit, all the time that he doeth it, his soul becometh weighed down with sin; but, if he deemeth justly of his own merit, or if he rate it lower than it is, then I, the Creator, will make his soul know joy and paradise, eternal brightness...and eternal happiness.

Judaism

When pride comes, then comes disgrace; but with the humble is wisdom.

Christianity

He who is greatest among you shall be your servant; whoever exalts himself will be humbled, and whoever humbles himself will be exalted.

"God opposes the proud but gives grace to the humble." Submit yourselves, therefore, to God...Humble yourselves before the Lord, and He will exalt you.

Islam

Walk not in the earth exultantly; God loves not any man proud and boastful.

But those who believe, and do righteous deeds, and have humbled themselves unto their Lord — they shall be the inhabitants of Paradise, therein dwelling forever.

PERSONAL NOTES

Chapter Sixteen

OBEDIENCE

Hinduism

After many births and deaths, he who is actually in knowledge surrenders unto
Me, knowing Me to be the cause of all causes and all that is.
Such a great soul is very rare.

Buddhism

One should follow dharma [the Law, the Truth, the Scripture],
which is good conduct,
Not that which is poor conduct.
One who lives dharma sleeps at ease
In this world and also in the next.

Taoism

He who acts in accordance with Tao becomes one with Tao...The man who is
one with Tao, Tao is also glad to receive.

If leaders could keep its [the Tao's] simplicity,
Then all people would honor and obey them.
Heaven and earth would combine to produce a sweet dew,
Which would fall, beyond anyone's command, equally on all men.

Confucianism

Confucius said, "If you are personally upright, things get done without any
orders being given. If you are not personally upright, no one will obey even if
you do give orders."

Zoroastrianism

I will speak the words which the Most Holy Wise Lord
Has told me are the best for mankind to hear:
"Those who for Me shall give heed and obedience to him [Zoroaster],
Shall attain Integrity and Immortality through the deeds of Good Mind."

Judaism

When you are in tribulation, and all these things come upon you in the latter days, you will return to the Lord, your God, and obey His voice; for the Lord, your God, is a merciful God...

Christianity

As obedient children, do not conform to the passions of your former ignorance, but as He Who called you is holy, be holy yourselves in all your conduct, since it is written, "You shall be holy, for I am holy."

Islam

Whosoever submits his will to God, being a good-doer,
his wage is with his Lord,
and no fear shall be on him, nor shall he sorrow.

PERSONAL NOTES

Chapter Seventeen

DUTY

Hinduism

One who performs his duty without attachment, surrendering the results unto the Supreme Lord, is unaffected by sinful action, as the lotus leaf is untouched by water.

Let even a youth accustom himself to do his duty, for life is frail. Fulfilled duty brings honor on earth and bliss in the world beyond.

Buddhism

If one's body and mind are under control, he should give evidence of it in virtuous deeds. This is a sacred duty...and to accumulate virtues will be his sacred task.

Taoism

The middle way is the duty of man. He should avoid all excess. In this way he fulfills his duty toward man and God.

Confucianism

The Master said, "Let the will be set on the path of duty.
"Let every attainment in what is good be firmly grasped.
"Let perfect virtue be accorded with..."

Zoroastrianism

The duty and good works which a son performs are as much the father's as though they had been done by his own hand.

Judaism

Fear God, and keep his commandments; for this is the whole duty of man.

Christianity

When you have done all that is commanded you, say, "We are unworthy servants; we have only done what was our duty."

Islam

All men who do their duty will receive a fitting reward from the Lord.

PERSONAL NOTES

Chapter Eighteen

WORK

Hinduism

And live in action! Labor! Make thine acts thy piety, casting all self aside,
condemning gain and merit...

Do thine allotted task! Work is more excellent than idleness; the body's life proceeds not, lacking work. There is a task of holiness to do, unlike world-binding toil, which bindeth not the faithful soul; such earthly duty do free from desire, and thou shalt well perform thy heavenly purpose.

Buddhism

Works, and not birth, determine one's place in the world. At all times one should work diligently and with earnestness. Hard work is praised.

Taoism

He [the sage] works without holding on,
Accomplishes without claiming merit.
Because he does not claim merit,
His merit does not go away.

Confucianism

Confucius said, "If you love people, can you let them not work?"

Zoroastrianism

He who, belonging to family or village or tribe, O Lord,
Is most good to the righteous man, or labors for the care of the herd,
He shall be in the pasture of Righteousness and of Good Mind.

Judaism

When you reap your harvest in your field and have forgotten a sheaf in the
field, you shall not go back to get it; it shall be for the sojourner, the fatherless,
and the widow, that the Lord, your God, may bless you
in all the work of your hands.

Christianity

Do not labor for the food which perishes, but for the food which endures to
eternal life...

Islam

"Work, and God will surely see your work...and you will be returned to Him
Who knows the unseen and the visible, and He will tell you
what you were doing."

PERSONAL NOTES

Chapter Nineteen

DEEDS

Hinduism

But thou, want not! Ask not! Find full reward of doing right in right! Let right deeds be thy motive, not the fruit which comes from them.

Buddhism

On the journey of life faith is nourishment, virtuous deeds are a shelter...

Taoism

Understand the value of action without deeds.
Teaching without words and the value of action without deeds
Are attained by very few. Deal with difficult things with simple acts.

Confucianism

The Master said, "See what a man does. Mark his motives..."

Zoroastrianism

Of the mind, good thoughts; of the tongue, good words;
Of the hand, good works; these make the virtuous life.

The Good Dominion must be man's choice;
It brings the most precious fate to him who acts with zeal.
Through the Right shall he attain the sovereign good for his deeds,
O Wise One.

Judaism

For God will bring every deed into judgment, with every secret thing, whether good or evil.

Requite them according to the work of their hands; render them their due reward.

Christianity

Who is wise and understanding among you? By his good life let him show his works in the meekness of wisdom.

For He will render to every man according to his works...

Islam

Whoso brings a good deed shall have ten the like of it, and whoso brings an evil deed shall only be recompensed the like of it; they shall not be wronged.

And those that believe, and do deeds of righteousness — those are the inhabitants of Paradise; there they shall dwell forever.

PERSONAL NOTES

Chapter Twenty

JUSTICE

Hinduism

The one who hurts pious men falls victim to his own designs.
This is divine justice.

Buddhism

The wise man weighs matters carefully so that he may judge justly.
Hasty judgment shows a man to be a fool.

Taoism

The Tao of heaven has no partiality;
It is always with the good people.

Confucianism

Confucius said, "The way ideal people relate to the world is to avoid both rejection and attachment. To treat others justly is their way of association."

Zoroastrianism

Toward the wicked man and the righteous one
And him in whom right and wrong meet
Shall the judge act in upright manner,
According to the laws of the present existence.

Judaism

From the Lord a man gets justice. An unjust man is an abomination to the righteous, but he whose way is straight is an abomination to the wicked.

Christianity

"Judge not, that you be not judged. For with the judgment you pronounce you will be judged, and the measure you give will be the measure you get."

Islam

Surely God bids to justice and good-doing and giving to kinsmen; and He forbids indecency, dishonor, and insolence, admonishing you, so that haply you will remember.

PERSONAL NOTES

Chapter Twenty-One

FORGIVENESS

Hinduism

God will forgive the sinner, if he earnestly casts away his sin. Human forgiveness is the way to happiness among men; a wise man will always be ready to forgive.

Buddhism

If a man possesses a repentant spirit, his sins will disappear; but if he has an unrepentant spirit, his sins will continue, and he must be condemned.

Taoism

With the faithful I would keep faith; with the unfaithful I would also keep faith, in order that they may become faithful.

Even if a man is bad, how can it be right to cast him off?

Requite injury with kindness.

Confucianism

One should forgive if the act is unintentional, but one should punish the intentional evil act.

Zoroastrianism

If one accepts and not the other, he who refuseth is at fault. If both accept, there is no fault.

Judaism

Who is a God like Thee, pardoning iniquity and passing over transgression for the remnant of His inheritance? He does not retain his anger forever, because He delights in steadfast love. He will again have compassion upon us; He will tread our iniquities underfoot.

Christianity

For if you forgive men their trespasses, your Heavenly Father also will forgive you; but if you do not forgive men their trespasses, neither will your Father forgive your trespasses.

Islam

But whoso repents after his evildoing and makes amends, God will turn toward him. Knowest thou not that to God belongs the kingdom of the heavens and the earth? He chastises whom He will and forgives whom He will; God is powerful over everything.

PERSONAL NOTES

Chapter Twenty-Two

PROSPERITY

Hinduism

What mortal dares to attack one who is rich in Thee?

When we die, the money and jewels that we have taken such trouble to amass during our life remain in the house...but our virtues and our vices follow us beyond the grave.

Buddhism

Desire for wealth and love...are not the eternal treasures. Enlightenment is the only treasure that holds its value.

Taoism

To accumulate wealth and treasures in excess,
This is called robbery and crime.
This is not to follow Tao.

One who knows contentment is rich.

Confucianism

Confucius said, "Wealth and rank are desired by people, but they do not remain if they are not obtained in the right way."

Virtue is the root; wealth is the result.

Zoroastrianism

How is he to obtain the cattle that brings prosperity, O Wise One,
He who desires it, together with its pastures?
Those who, among the many that behold the sun,
Live uprightly, according to Righteousness.

Judaism

Help us to see that no work truly prospers unless it brings blessing to other lives, and that no gain truly enriches if it adds not to the happiness of others...Help us so to live that, when we shall have gathered our final harvest, many shall rise up and call us blessed.

Christianity

"Do not lay up for yourselves treasures on earth, where moths and rust consume and where thieves break in and steal, but lay up for yourselves treasures in heaven, where neither moths nor rust consumes and where thieves do not break in and steal. For where your treasure is, there will your heart be, also."

As for the rich in this world, charge them...not to set their hopes on uncertain riches but on God, Who richly furnishes us with everything to enjoy. They are to do good, to be rich in good deeds, liberal and generous, thus laying up for themselves a good foundation for the future, so that they may take hold of the life that is life indeed.

Islam

And whosoever is guarded against the avarice of his own soul,
those — they are the prosperers.

Whatever thing you have been given is for the enjoyment of the present life, but
what is with God is better and more enduring for those who believe and put
their trust in their Lord.

Chapter Twenty-Three

HUMAN
AND
DIVINE

Hinduism

When the fruit grows, the petals drop off of themselves.
So when the Divinity in thee increases, the weakness of humanity
in thee will vanish.

Buddhism

It need not take long to learn the Buddha's teachings, for all humans possess a
nature that has affinity for enlightenment.

Buddha is one who has attained Buddhahood; people are those who are capable
of attaining Buddhahood. That is all the difference there is between them.

Taoism

Man is both human and divine. The divine in him is eternal and of infinite
worth. The human may pass away, but the divine is everlasting.
His goodness comes from God.

He who knows what it is that heaven does, and knows what it is that man does,
has reached the peak. Knowing what it is that heaven does, he lives with
heaven. Knowing what it is that man does, he uses the knowledge of
what he knows to help out the knowledge of what he doesn't know...
this is the perfection of knowledge.

Confucianism

He who gets to the bottom of his mind comes to know his own nature; knowing
his own nature, he also knows God. Preserving one's mind in its integrity and
nourishing one's nature is the way to serve God.

Zoroastrianism

The Wise One created man to be like Him. The mind of man enclosed in a body comes from the divine. Thus, man should serve only the good and flee from all that is wicked.

Judaism

When I look at Thy heavens, the work of Thy fingers, the moon and the stars which Thou hast established — what is man that Thou art mindful of him and the son of man that Thou dost care for him? Yet Thou hast made him little less than God and dost crown him with glory and honor. Thou hast given him dominion over the works of Thy hands...

Christianity

God has revealed to us through the Spirit. For the Spirit searches everything, even the depths of God. For what person knows a man's thoughts except the spirit of the man which is in him? So also no one comprehends the thoughts of God except the Spirit of God. Now we have received not the spirit of the world, but the Spirit which is from God, that we might understand the gifts bestowed on us by God. And we impart this in words not taught by human wisdom but taught by the Spirit, interpreting spiritual truths to those who possess the Spirit.

Islam

Why, surely, to God belongs whatsoever is in the heavens and the earth. He always knows what state you are in; the day when you shall be returned to Him, then He will tell you of what you did; God knows everything.

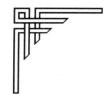

PERSONAL NOTES

Chapter Twenty-Four

IMMORTALITY

Hinduism

Never the Spirit was born;
The Spirit shall cease to be never;
Never was time it was not;
End and beginning are dreams!

Birthless and deathless and changeless
Remaineth the Spirit forever;
Death hath not touched It at all,
Dead though the house of It seems!

Buddhism

By faith you shall be free and go beyond the realm of death.

Taoism

Birth is not a beginning; death is not an end.

To have attained to the human form must be always a source of joy. And then, to undergo countless transitions, with only the infinite to look forward to — what incomparable bliss is that! Thus it is that the truly wise rejoice in that which can never be lost but endures always.

Confucianism

You do not understand life; how can you understand death?...
Death and life are as decreed.

Zoroastrianism

This I ask Thee, O Lord --- answer me truly:
Shall I attain my goal with You, O Wise One?
May I become one with You and may my word have power,
That Integrity and Immortality according to Thy order
May join themselves with the follower of Righteousness.

To him who is Thy true friend in spirit and in actions,
O Mazda Ahura [the Creator],
To him Thou shalt give a good life and immortality;
To him Thou shalt give perpetual communion with Truth and
the Kingdom of Heaven,
And to him Thou shalt give the sustaining strength
of the Good Mind [Providence].

Judaism

Dust we are, and unto dust we return, but the spirit born of Thy Spirit,
breathed into the clay to animate and to ennoble,
returns unto Thee, the Fountainhead of all spirits...
Teach us to acknowledge Thy sovereignty and Thy wisdom with perfect trust
that death is but the portal unto eternal life.

Christianity

For He will render to every man according to his works: to those who by
patience in well-doing seek for glory and honor and immortality,
He will give eternal life...

How do you disbelieve in God, seeing you were dead and He gave you life,
then He shall make you dead, then He shall give you life,
then unto Him you shall be returned?

AFTERWORD

Posed at the beginning of this work were questions that these sacred writings were selected to illumine. And yet, perhaps this exploration has prompted even more questions to be contemplated.

Why has the Parent God allowed such a variety of religions to exist? Why has He sent different masters in different ages? Is it that humankind can only understand and profoundly integrate certain truths at certain times in history? Like any wise and compassionate parent, does God give us, his children, only the guidance we are ready for and can handle at each stage of our development? Does the Divine Will change as we grow and change? Jesus taught in parables, because he said that the people of his time could not hear the entire truth if he spoke it plainly.

Has humankind been evolving spiritually? Will it continue to evolve, and will new masters be needed and emerge to continue the work of their forebears and to guide us even further toward our spiritual destiny?

BIBLIOGRAPHY

General Reference

Editorial staff of *Life* magazine. *The World's Great Religions: Vol.1: Religions of the East.* New York: Time, Inc., 1963.

Finegan, Jack. *The Archeology of World Religions.* Princeton, NJ: Princeton University Press, 1952.

Ghai, O.P. *Unity in Diversity.* New Delhi: Institute of Personal Development, 1986.

Lyon, Quinter Marcellus. *The Great Religions.* New York: The Odyssey Press, Inc., 1957.

Noss, John B. *Man's Religions.* 3d ed. New York: The Macmillan Company, 1963.

Oriental Treasures. Kansas City, MO: Hallmark Cards, Inc., 1967.

Springs of Oriental Wisdom. New York: Herder Book Center, 1964.

Hinduism

Brown, Brian. *The Wisdom of the Hindus.* Albuquerque, NM: Sun Books, 1981.

His Divine Grace A.C. Bhaktivedanta Swami Prabhupada. *Bhagavad-Gita As It Is.* Vaduz, Lichtenstein: The Bhaktivedanta Book Trust, 1983.

Pereira, Jose, ed. *Hindu Theology: A Reader.* Garden City, NY: Image Books, 1976.

Swami Nikhilananda, ed. and trans. *The Uphanishads.* New York:
Harper & Row, Publishers, 1964.

Buddhism

Bukkyo Dendo Kyokai. *The Teaching of Buddha.* Tokyo:
Bukkyo Dendo Kyokai, 1971.

Carter, John Ross, and Mahinda Palihawadana, trans. *The Dhammapada.*
New York: Oxford University Press, 1987.

Conze, Edward. *Buddhism: Its Essence and Development.* New York:
Harper & Row, Publishers, 1965.

---, trans. *Buddhist Scriptures.* Baltimore, MD: Penguin Books, 1971.

---, ed. in collaboration with I.B. Horner, D. Snellgrove, A. Waley. *Buddhist Texts
Through the Ages.* New York: Harper & Row, Publishers, 1964.

Thomas, E. J., trans. *Buddhist Scriptures.* The Wisdom of the East Series. ed.
L. Cranmer-Byng and Dr. S. A. Kapadia. London: John Murray, 1913.

---, ed. and trans. *Early Buddhist Scriptures.* London: Kegan Paul, Trench, Trubner
& Co., Ltd., 1935.

Warren, Henry Clarke, trans. *Buddhism in Translations.* New York:
Atheneum, 1963.

Taoism

Chen, Ellen M., trans. *The Tao Te Ching.* New York:
Paragon House, 1989.

Dalton, Jerry O. *The Tao Te Ching, Backward Down the Path.* Atlanta: Humanics Limited, 1994.

Giles, Lionel, trans. *Musings of a Chinese Mystic,* Selections From the Philosophy of Chuang Tzu. The Wisdom of the East Series. ed. L. Cranmer-Byng and Dr. S. A. Kapadia. London: John Murray, 1911.

---, trans. *The Sayings of Lao-Tzu.* The Wisdom of the East Series. ed. L. Cranmer-Byng. London: John Murray, 1950.

Grigg, Ray. *The Tao of Relationships.* Atlanta: Humanics Limited, 1988.

Merton, Thomas. *The Way of Chuang Tzu.* New York: New Directions, 1965.

Watson, Burton, trans. *Chuang Tzu: Basic Writings.* Translations from the Oriental Classics. ed. William Theodore De Bary. New York: Columbia University Press, 1964.

Confucianism

Bahm, Archie J. *The Heart of Confucius: Interpretations of <u>Genuine Living</u> (Chung Yung) and <u>Great Wisdom</u> (Ta Hsueh).* New York: Walker/Weatherhill, 1969.

Chai, Ch'u, and Winberg Chai, eds. and trans. *The Sacred Books of Confucius.* New York: Bantam Books, Inc., 1965.

Cleary, Thomas, trans. *The Essential Confucius: The Heart of Confucius' Teachings in Authentic I Ching Order.* New York: HarperCollins Publishers, 1993.

Creel, H. G. *Confucius and the Chinese Way.* New York: Harper & Row, Publishers, 1949.

Giles, Lionel, trans. *The Book of Mencius* (abridged). The Wisdom of the East Series. ed. L. Cranmer-Byng and Alan W. Watts. London: John Murray, 1942.

Legge, James, trans. *The Philosophy of Confucius*. New York: The Peter Pauper Press, 1963.

Zoroastrianism

Darmesteter, James, trans. *The Zend-Avesta*. 2d ed. Oxford: Clarendon Press, 1895.

Dawson, Miles Menander. *The Ethical Religion of Zoroaster*. New York: The Macmillan Company, 1931.

Duchesne-Guillemin, French trans. (English trans. from French by Mrs. M. Henning). *The Hymns of Zarathustra*. Boston: Beacon Press, 1963.

Kotwal, Firoze M., and James W. Boyd, eds. and trans. *A Guide to the Zoroastrian Religion*. Chico, California: Scholars Press, 1982.

Masani, Sir Rustom. *The Religion of the Good Life: Zoroastrianism*. London: George Allen & Unwin Ltd., 1954.

Judaism

May, Herbert G., and Bruce M. Metzger, eds. *The New Oxford Annotated Bible With The Apocrypha*. Revised Standard Version. New York: Oxford University Press, 1977.

The Central Conference of American Rabbis, ed. *The Union Prayer Book for Jewish Worship*. Newly Revised Edition. Part I. Cincinnati: The Central Conference of American Rabbis, 1954.

110

Christianity

May, Herbert G., and Bruce M. Metzger, eds. *The New Oxford Annotated Bible With Apocrypha.* Revised Standard Version. New York: Oxford University Press, 1977.

Islam

Arberry, Arthur J., trans. *The Koran Interpreted.* New York: The Macmillan Company, 1955.

PERSONAL NOTES

PERSONAL NOTES

PERSONAL NOTES

PERSONAL NOTES

PERSONAL NOTES

PERSONAL NOTES

PERSONAL NOTES